Rainfore

written by Kelly Gaffney

Rainforests are wonderful places,
filled with plants and animals.
Rainforests are always wet because it rains
almost every day.

Rainforests are beautiful and green.
There are plants everywhere.
They grow on the ground, on rocks
and even on other plants!
Some of the plants that grow
in the rainforest are large,
while others are tiny.

The tops of the tallest trees are called
the *canopy* of the rainforest.
The trees in the canopy give shade
to the plants growing below.

The plants that do not reach the top
of the canopy are called the *understorey.*
They are often covered in *moss* and *vines*.

The ground below the trees is called the *forest floor.*
The forest floor is very *shady.*
The ground is covered with leaves, and it is very muddy.

canopy
understorey
forest floor

vine
moss

Many wonderful plants grow in the rainforest.
The world's biggest flower grows in the rainforest.
It is huge and smells terrible!

Some plants in the rainforest grow on the trees.
These plants catch water in their leaves when it rains.

Other plants get their food from the trees
that they grow on.
Some plants even get their food by eating *insects*
and small animals!

Many different animals live in the rainforest, too.
Lots of these animals don't live anywhere else
in the world.
The rainforest is home to frogs, snakes and birds.
Big cats and monkeys can live in rainforests, too.

Some rainforest animals live up in the trees.
They don't come down to the ground very often.
These animals find the food they need
among the branches.
They drink the rain that falls onto the leaves.

Many rainforest animals are very colourful.
Some birds have colourful *beaks*,
while others have colourful *feathers*.

The frogs in the rainforest can be very colourful, too.
Some are red, yellow or bright green.
There are even blue frogs in some rainforests!

You can find lots of wonderful insects and spiders in the rainforest.
One of the biggest spiders in the world lives in the rainforest.
This spider can grow as big as a dinner plate.
It eats insects, frogs and even small birds.

The rainforest is also home
to the world's biggest butterfly.
This butterfly has bright green, black and yellow wings.

Rainforests are very special places,
but they could be gone one day.
People are cutting down the trees to use the wood.
The wood from the trees is used to build things.
When the forest is cut down, the animals
have nowhere to go.

Rainforests are important places, so we need
to protect them.

Picture glossary

beaks

forest floor

shady

canopy

insects

understorey

feathers

moss

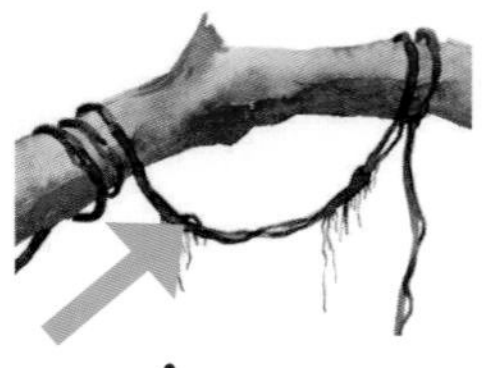

vines